All Across EUROPE

Ellen Weisberg and
Ken Yoffe

Published by Waldorf Publishing

2140 Hall Johnson Road

#102-345

Grapevine, Texas 76051

www.WaldorfPublishing.com

All Across Europe

ISBN: 978-1-64255-778-7

Library of Congress Control Number: 2018933240

Copyright © 2019

We thank the following friends and family for their valuable feedback: Martin Sattler, Sigrun Leonhardt, Elke Raderschall, Lizi and Jenny Wu, Kenny Colville, Frank Williams, Dee Cohen, Kelly and Peter Gousios and family, Mary Small, Cindy Brunelle, Jennifer Metcalf, Holly Pettit, Leona Palmer, Gina Rosati, Maria Hubert, Marie Mueller, Chu Chen, Joseph Weisberg, and Irwin Weisberg

We thank our family and friends...

Sheila Weisberg, Larry Weisberg, Judi Klevan, Victor Gold, Aimee Lyndon-Adams, Ann Kushner, David, Noah and Andy Kushner, Mike and Sue Villeco, Ronnie and Esta Joy Kroten, Ellen and George Munk, Charlie Munk, Amy Rodriguez, Mae Gold, Dan and Susan Acker, David and Eva Acker, Joel and Tara Acker, Estelle and Jerry Altman, Rachel Acker and Brian Beduhn and Rosie and Annabelle, Jane Yoffe, Jonathan and Annette Yoffe, Sonya Hutchens, Karen Sclare and Harvey Yoffe.

Suzanne Meyer, Barbara Segal, Tim Mello, Lisa Kallianidis, Deb Daigle, Franny and Jake Wolf, Dee Cohen, Elizabeth Cohen, Diane Marotta, Judy Moore, Shari Ostrowsky, Rhodella Hughes, Fay McDaniel, Julie Langbort, Sharon Midlin-Levy, Cynthia Horowitz, Rob Orkovitz, Amy Slutsky SklarRenee Wright, Lolita Banerji, Marie-Terese Little, Bill Richter, Cara Cavazza, Rosemary Barrett, Arghya Ray, Jingrui Jiang, Chengcheng Meng, Christian Sillaber, Dorna Baumann, Laura and Larry Fitzgerald, Elizabeth Curry, Joanne Choi, Tom Finocchiaro, Randall Rosenbaum, Suzanne Katz, Kira Sekulow, David Gracer, Christopher Scott Martin and Kim Calcagno, Maggie and Wren St. Germain, Karla Gregory, Julie and Scott Zimmett, Paul Kravitz, John Schrader, Kristen Kerouac, Rosalie Nesbit, Lynette King, Jon and Marilyn Volovick, Hiroko Kishikawa, Maggie Dean, Alexandra Wischnewski, Brenda Silver, Ann Penta, Keith Tan, Jose Veliz, Michelle Newell, Amy Sheldon-Calzonetti, Danielle Love, Lea Hope Becker, Shameme Adams, Gary Sohmers, Jon Marable, Rob Carolan, Gary Best, Rob St. Pierre, Mike and Stacy Smalley, Denise Youseff, Dan Walsh, Dave and Natalie Salamon, Beth Atkins, Jake and Connie Guralnick, and Rafael Pabon.

Special thanks to Dr. James Griffin

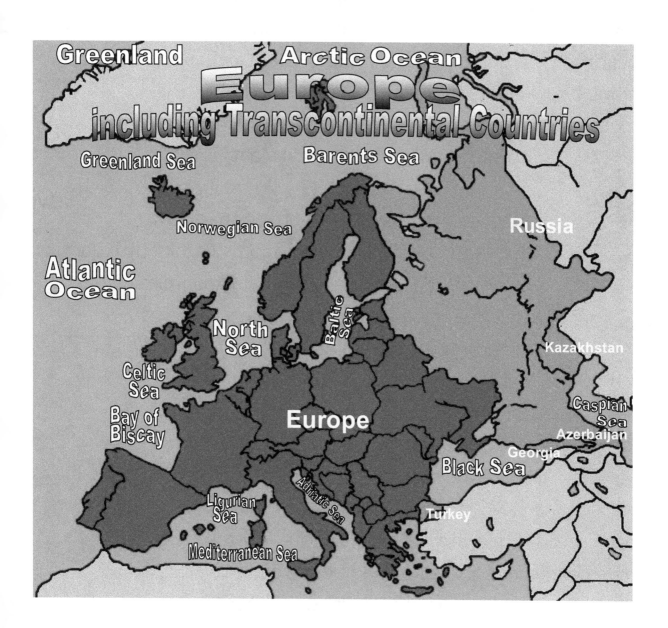

Welcome...

... to the fascinating continent of Europe! With at least 48 countries, and probably more joining some day, it is home to over 800 million people from hundreds of cultural backgrounds. Europe is also home to animals of all sizes and shapes, and beautiful mountains and rivers. It is full of impressive structures to see and delicious food to eat, as well!

Stevie

Most of the countries in Europe are on the mainland, which stretches from the North Atlantic Ocean in the west to the Ural Mountains of Russia in the east, and from the frigid Arctic Ocean north of Norway to the Mediterranean Sea down south.

Wendy

These "mainland" countries are divided into Eastern, Northern, Southern, Central, and Western regions. This is where three of our friends- Ernie, Stevie, and Wendy- will take you on an exploration! And remember, in each country they visit, they have a pal that just so happens to be named after the capital of that country (like Little Rome, who lives in Italy).

Ernie

Wait! There's more...

Western Europe is also where six microstates (small republics or principalities) are found. These interesting countries are among the smallest in the world. Most are merely the size of large towns! As a special treat, your buddy, Mickey, will take you on a quick journey through these wonderful places.

Mickey

A country can be part of Europe, even if it does not lie entirely on the mainland. For example, the island countries of Iceland, Ireland, and the United Kingdom are located in Western Europe, although they are not on the mainland. Many people who live in these places don't consider themselves to be "Mainland Europeans."

Other examples are the transcontinental countries, which lie partly in Europe and partly in the continent of Asia to the east. In the case of Russia, most of the country is in Asia. However, its European part alone would be the largest country in Europe! Your pal, Tricia, will finish your travels with a tour of these fine countries.

Tricia

One more thing!

As you shall see, we have divided Europe into several regions (such as Central Europe). In most cases, these regions are simply groups of countries that lie near each other, and these groupings provide a way to help learn where each country of Europe is located. These regions do not necessarily assemble countries that are alike in their geography, politics, or culture, although many of them do share similarities.

In fact, others place some countries in different regions than are shown here. For example, Germany could correctly be considered a Central, Western, or Northern European country. Plus, there are some countries, such as Armenia and Cyprus, which are not considered to be part of European geography but play important roles in European culture and politics.

And the number of countries in Europe still seems to be growing!

One example is Kosovo, which is located in Southern Europe.

Western, Northern, Eastern, Central and Southern Europe

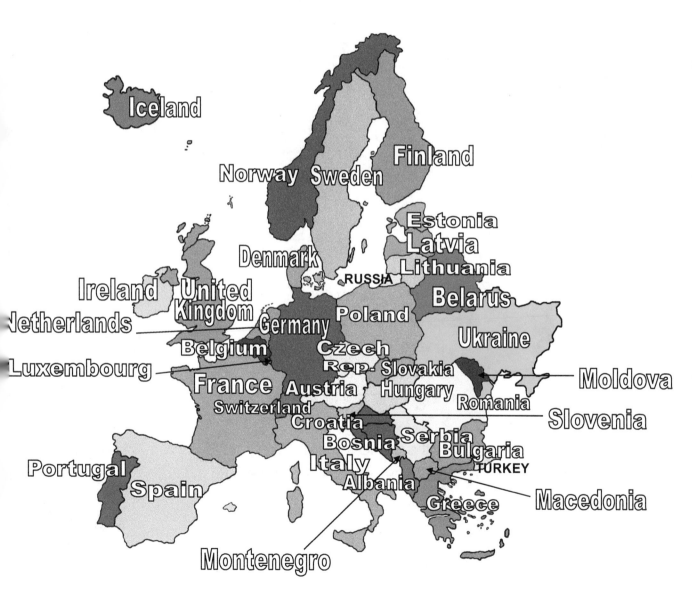

Ernie hikes the Swedish hills
in the chilly regions north,
while Stevie climbs the southern Alps,
and continues moving forth.
Wendy visits islands of
Great Britain in the west,
and settles up in Iceland
where she takes a needed rest.

The three are always moving
and are seeing many places.
There never is a shortage
of good meals and friendly faces.
Through the continent of Europe
they all happily will go
and they'll stop to spend some time with
special people that they know.

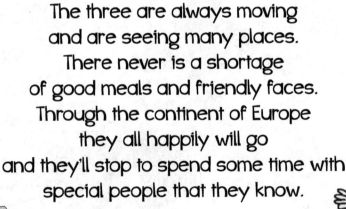

Seeing Central and Southern Europe with Stevie

Stevie takes a tasty trip,
through Europe's central part.
In Poland, there's pierogi,
and in Austria, Linzer tart.
Now that he is all fueled up
with tons of energy...
He heads right past the Balkan lakes ...
toward Greece, and Aegean Sea.

Central Europe

Baltic Sea

POLAND

CZECH REPUBLIC

SLOVAKIA

AUSTRIA

HUNGARY

Stevie

POLAND

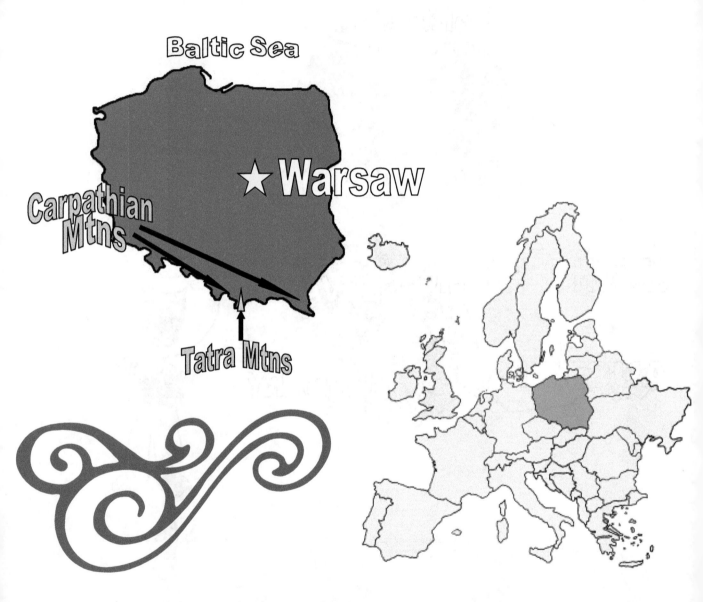

Baltic Sea

★ Warsaw

Carpathian Mtns

Tatra Mtns

The Tatra Mountains are Poland's highest point and are the highest mountain range of the Carpathians. Poland was home to composer Frederic Chopin and scientists Nicolaus Copernicus and Marie Sklodowska Curie.

Big bison called wisent
in forests will roam,
while migrating birds
make Poland their home.
Little Miss Warsaw
climbs dunes, past the lakes,
eating kielbasa
that her mother makes.
She thinks of her country
and is proud as can be...
the birthplace of great ones,
like Madame Curie.

Little Miss
Warsaw

CZECH REPUBLIC

☆Prague

Before the Velvet Revolution, a nonviolent transfer of power in 1989, the Czech Republic and Slovakia were once one country called Czechoslovakia.

Prague

Little Prague's a lucky boy
from high society.
The castles and chateaus he owns
are quite a sight to see.
His father works to entertain
and is a puppeteer.
Dad likes drinking after shows
some cold Budweis town beer.

SLOVAKIA

★Bratislava

Hockey is an important sport in Slovakia. Volkswagen cars originated in Germany, but some are produced in Slovakia.

Impish Bratislava is up to no good.
He's known just as "bratty" in his neighborhood.
He'd go run and hide in a castle or cave,
and jump out at people, and just misbehave.
His father, a maker of Volkswagen cars,
would insist that Bratty belonged behind bars!
But deep down he knew there was good in the lad.
He'd whisper in Slovak, "I was just as bad."

Bratislava

AUSTRIA

Vienna☆

Austria is home to composers Joseph Haydn and Johann Strauss. The Northern Alps of Austria are one of the homes of Alpine skiing.

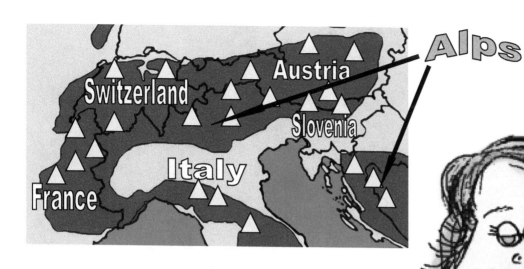

Vienna skis the eastern Alps
with foothills down below.
She speaks in German, her native tongue,
and greets folks she might know.
Wiener Schnitzel for lunch she eats
and Strudel to finish the meal.
She listens to Mozart to lull her to sleep.
So calm it makes her feel!

Vienna

HUNGARY

Hungary was once part of the Austro-Hungarian Empire, a union of the Austrian Empire and the Kingdom of Hungary. The Great Hungarian Plain is home to the largest grasslands in Europe.

Little Mr. Budapest

Budapest will often reflect
on the work of great, great men.
Among the finds are vitamin C,
fake blood and the ballpoint pen.
As festivals go, in the spring and fall,
his country has lots and lots.
They serve paprika and sour cream
and goulash in big steaming pots.

Southern Europe

SLOVENIA

CROATIA

BOSNIA AND HERZEGOVINA

Adriatic Sea

SERBIA

MONTENEGRO

MACEDONIA

ALBANIA

GREECE

Aegean Sea

Stevie

SLOVENIA

★Ljubljana

A "karst" landscape, which is full of caves and sinkholes, is named after the Karst plateau of southwest Slovenia and northeast Italy.

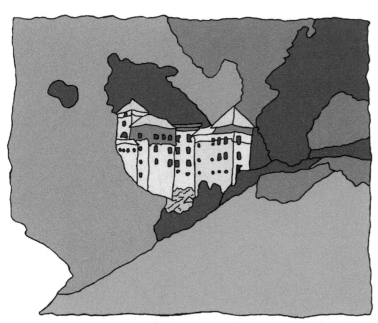

Little Miss Jana,
Slovene does she speak.
She lives on Mt. Triglav,
her home's highest peak.
She loves to ride horses
through trees made of pine,
past castles that take her
quite far back in time.
There are Alps in the north
and Karst in southwest.
Forests of oak
fill up much of the rest.

Little Miss Ljubljana
"Jana"

CROATIA

The Dinaric Alps are located in Croatia, as well as Slovenia, Bosnia, Serbia, Montenegro and Albania.

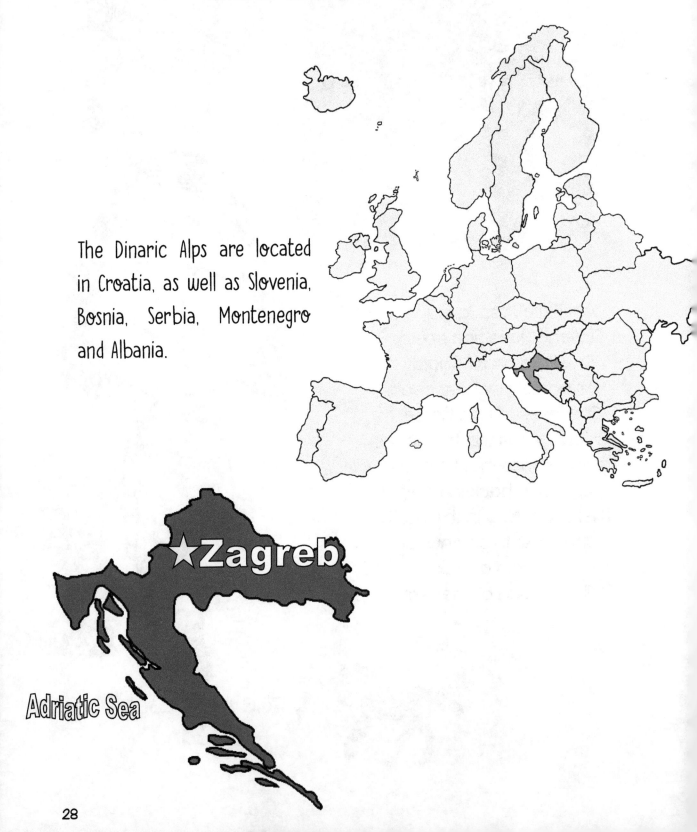

★Zagreb

Adriatic Sea

Zagreb climbs the rocky coast
and gazes at the seas.
He thinks of his Croatian land
and great discoveries.
The makers of the necktie were
the Croats of yesteryear.
Fountain pens as well were also
first invented here.

Zagreb

BOSNIA AND HERZEGOVINA

Bosnia is named after the Bosna River. The Sava River forms much of the northern border of Bosnia. Sarajevo once hosted the Olympics and is called "The Olympic City."

Sarajevo

Sarajevo lives up north,
a place where he grows crops.
When work is through, a coffee house
is where he often stops.
For fun he also likes to raft.
He often goes to ski.
There are lots of lovely waterfalls
for him to pass and see.

MONTENEGRO

★Podgorica

Adriatic
Sea

Montenegro, Serbia, Bosnia,
Croatia, Slovenia, and Macedonia
once comprised a single country
called Yugoslavia.

Little "Pod" strolls right past
the tallest of karst peaks.
He heads down toward the Port of Bar.
The seacoast's what he seeks.
Fine monuments and lovely towns
he passes on his way.
A folk dance and fish dinner will
both end his awesome day.

Little Mr. Podgorica
"Pod"

Kotor

Bar

Ulcinj

SERBIA

★Belgrade

Balkan Mtns

The Balkans region of Europe is named for the Balkan Mountains, which run through Bulgaria and Eastern Serbia. One-third of the world's raspberries are from Serbia!

Belgrade watches the great Danube flow
while he sits by the riverside.
The wetlands and parks are lovely to see.
The mountains stretch far and wide.
Raspberries grow in great supply.
His dad gathers many each day.
Then father and son take a ride into town
to watch an opera or play.

Little Mr. Belgrade

MACEDONIA

★Skopje

The country of Macedonia is not to be confused with the neighboring region of Macedonia in Greece. The Molika, or Macedonian Pine, is a very well known tree.

Skopje lives near a
huge, huge lake.
It's one of the oldest around!
Lake Ohrid's its name,
and it's down in the south.
In it, old snails can be found.
Big celebrations he likes to attend,
with jazz and great poems
and some drama.
He loves Shopska salad
when it is prepared
by his Macedonian mama.

Skopje

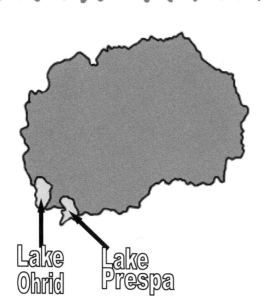

Lake
Ohrid   Lake
Prespa

ALBANIA

Adriatic
Sea

★Tirana

Ionian
Sea

Most of the population of
Albania is Muslim. Albania is a
major producer of figs.

Tirana dances along the coast
near the Ionian Sea.
Some bears and wolves and lynx all watch
from behind a huge Oak tree.
Way up over a deep Balkan lake,
a Golden Eagle so big,
flies past Tirana as she takes a rest
and munches on a fig.

Tirana

GREECE

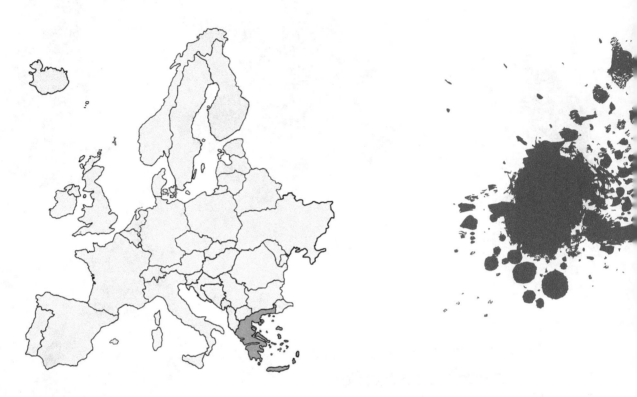

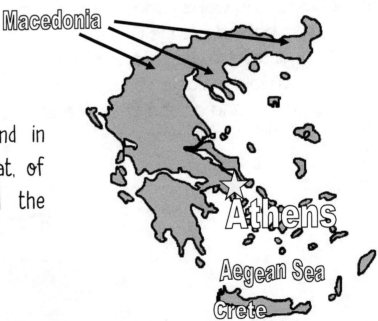

Macedonia

Athens

Aegean Sea

Crete

Crete is the largest island in Greece. Alexander the Great, of Greek Macedonia, created the Greek Empire around 300 BC.

Athens

At lunchtime Athens eats some greens
with olive oil, too.
She loves sweet spice like cinnamon
and cloves cooked into stew.
When Athens goes to school she learns
ideas of Socrates,
the Age of Gods and epic poems
like Homer's Odyssey.
A fine Greek play by Sophocles
is something she might see,
then back again to Plato for more
Greek philosophy.

Exploring Eastern and Northern Europe with Ernie

As Ernie travels toward the east,
a pack of wolves he'll pass.
There's nothing like a sight like that
to make a boy run fast!
Ernie walks the northern plain
and sails the Barents Sea.
He goes through Finland heading to
Helsinki and Mikkeli.

Eastern Europe

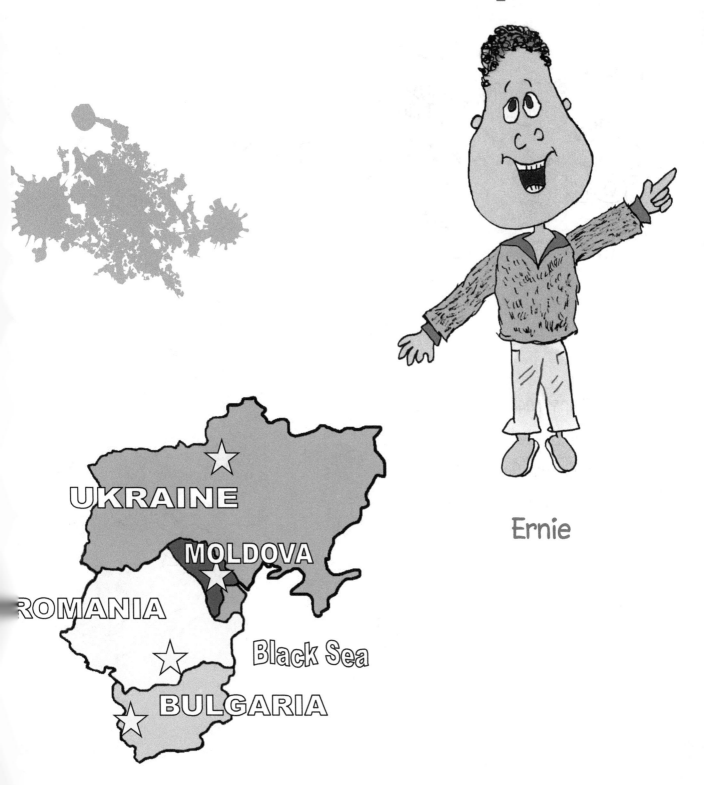

UKRAINE

MOLDOVA

ROMANIA

Black Sea

BULGARIA

Ernie

BULGARIA

Balkan Mtns

Black Sea

Sofia

The Balkans region of Europe, named for the Balkan Mountains, includes Albania, Greece, Bulgaria, and the six former Yugoslavian countries.

Sofia's dad's a miner
of copper, zinc and coal.
To export all that he can find
is her dad's biggest goal.
While daddy works, Sofia plays
in mountains filled with snow.
For warmth and sun, the Black Sea coast
is where she'll sometimes go.

COAL

Sofia

ROMANIA

Carpathian Mtns

Bucharest ☆ **Black Sea**

The Carpathian Mountains dominate central Romania. The real Dracula, or Vlad The Impaler, lived in a castle in Romania.

Through the trees a wolf is seen
as well as a big brown bear.
There are so many plants and flora around
some common and some quite rare.
In a place called "Bran," a castle sits.
It once was home to a queen.
It was also used by Dracula,
a prince who was really quite mean.

Little Bucharest

47

MOLDOVA

Chisinău★

Moldova, which previously belonged to the former Soviet Union, is known for its wines and rich soil that is great for agriculture.

Chis's mom and dad
make a living selling wine.
They run a little vineyard
and grow grapes that taste so fine.
Tobacco, fruits and vegetables
are other things they grow.
They like to walk the hills of the
Moldavian Plateau.

Chisinău
"Chis"

UKRAINE

The Ukraine was formerly in the Soviet Union.
The Easter Egg, or pysanki, is a very old and
important part of Ukranian culture.

The Carpathian Mountains
in western Ukraine,
are where Kiev heads
while walking the plain.
Her grandma cooks borscht
and Chicken Kiev, too.
She has some sweet kompot,
made of fruit that is stewed.

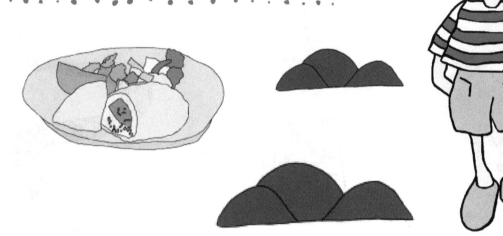

Little Miss Kiev

Northern Europe

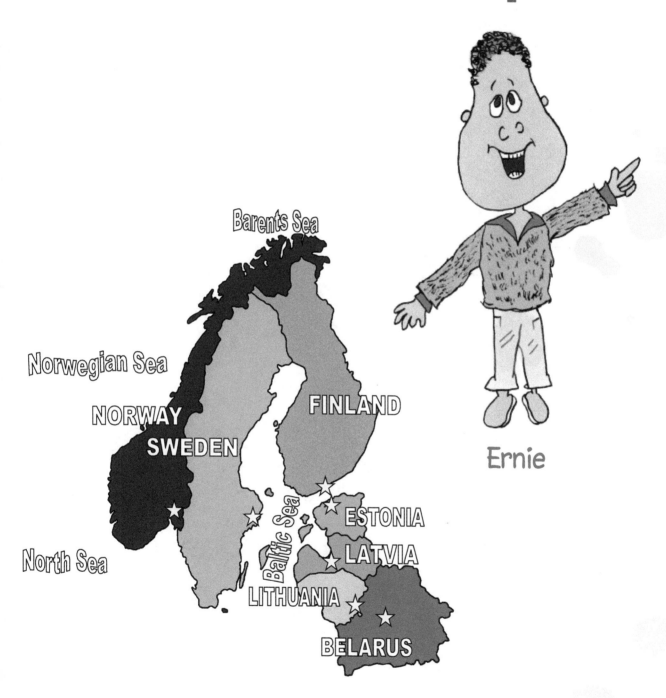

Barents Sea

Norwegian Sea

NORWAY

SWEDEN

FINLAND

North Sea

Baltic Sea

ESTONIA

LATVIA

LITHUANIA

BELARUS

Ernie

BELARUS

Belarus was formerly in the Soviet Union. The national dish of Belarus is Draniki, or potato pancakes.

Minsk is nice and toasty warm,
with clothing made of wool.
A bunch of shirts and pants of flax
does keep his wardrobe full.
His dad will fish the many lakes,
and bring back eel to eat.
Pork is cooked and served as well,
with salted bread a treat.

Minsk

LITHUANIA

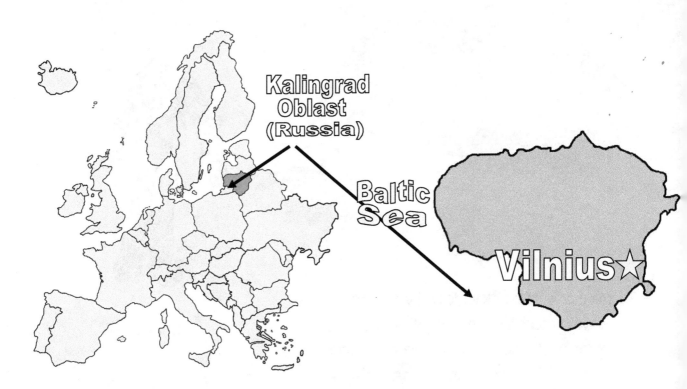

Furniture production is a growing and important part of the economy. South of Lithuania is the Kalingrad Oblast, a small part of Russia, separated from the rest of the country.

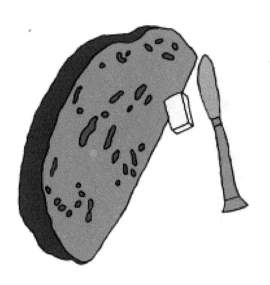

Vilnius eats a big dark slice of
rye bread spread with butter.
She also likes the kreplach and the kugel
made by mother.
The wetlands and the lakes and
tiny coastline by the sea
are all the things that she will say
make up her fine country.

Little Miss
Vilnius

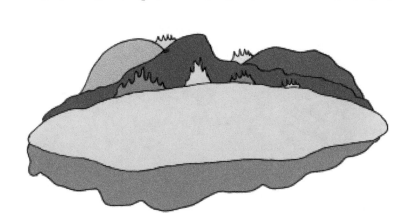

LATVIA

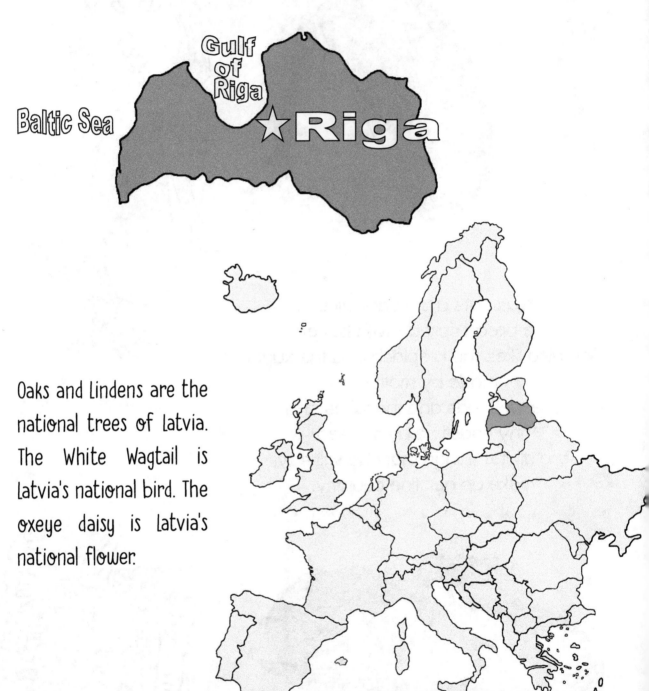

Gulf of Riga

Baltic Sea

★Riga

Oaks and Lindens are the national trees of Latvia. The White Wagtail is Latvia's national bird. The oxeye daisy is Latvia's national flower.

Little Riga walks the plains
through forests made of pine.
Oaks and Lindens dot her path,
with daisies looking fine.
The gulf appears and is a sight
hard to describe with words.
She sees up high a white wagtail,
one of her favorite birds.

Little Miss Riga

ESTONIA

Tallinn

Baltic Sea

Estonia, Latvia, and Lithuania are called the Baltic States, and were previously part of the Soviet Union. 50% of Estonia is covered by forest.

Tallinn lives on the northern coast
along the Baltic Sea.
He goes southeast for winter months
where snow climbs to his knee.
He visits many lakes and bogs.
The rivers are a thrill.
He catches fish and hunts for game
and cooks it on a grill.

Tallinn

FINLAND

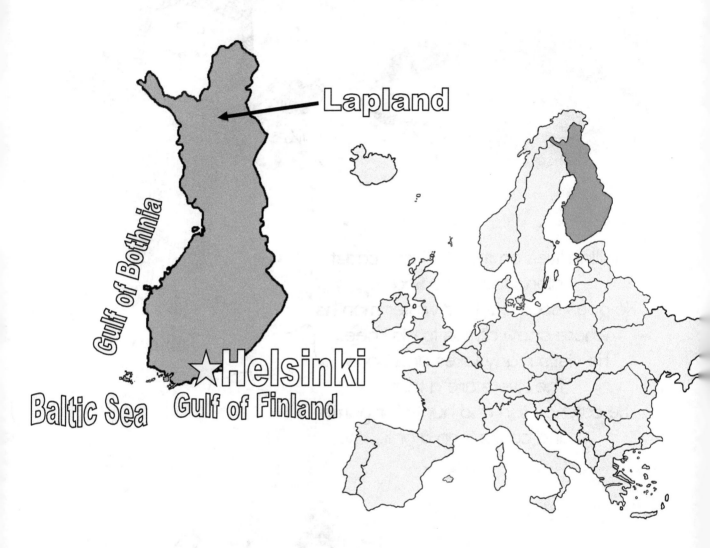

Lapland

Gulf of Bothnia

Baltic Sea

★Helsinki

Gulf of Finland

Lapland is considered by many to be the traditional home of Father Christmas. Some of the world's biggest cruise ships are built in Finland.

Little Miss Helsinki

Helsinki tries to not be bad
and follow all the laws.
She knows that northern Lapland
is the home to Santa Claus.
So many lakes and islands
for her friends to find and search.
Big cruise ships they see far away
through woods of pine and birch.

SWEDEN

Stockholm ☆

Gulf of Bothnia

Baltic Sea

The Scandinavian Peninsula is made up of Norway and Sweden. However, the area known as "Scandinavia" also includes Finland and Denmark. The Nobel Prize was first established in Sweden.

ake Vänern

Oland

Gotland

Little Mr.
Stockholm

Stockholm's Swedish meatballs
taste so tangy in his mouth.
They're part of a big Smörgåsbord
served at his farm down south.
To huge Lake Vänern he will go,
when finished with his feast.
Then he'll head toward Gotland,
a large island in the east.
He thinks about the arctic north
and sun that does not rise.
He also dreams of winning big,
perhaps a Nobel prize.

Svalbard

NORWAY

Norwegian Sea

★ Oslo

North Sea

Hornindalsvatnet is the deepest lake in Europe. Norway and Sweden make up the Scandinavian Peninsula.

Lake Hornindalsvatnet

Oslo

Oslo walks along the coast
that's filled with fjords so steep.
So many glaciers are around,
and a lake that's oh so deep.
Oslo's from a wealthy kin.
His dad sells fish and oil.
He loves his peaceful, lovely land.
To Norway he is loyal.

Wandering Through Western Europe with Wendy

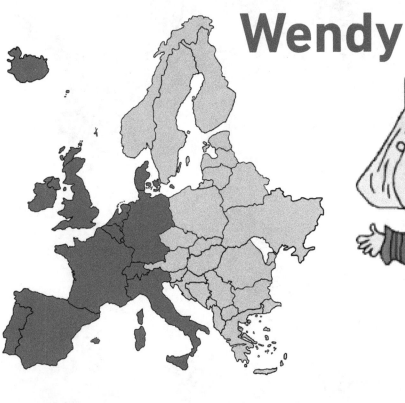

Wendy walks through wooded land,
and climbs a big beech tree.
She then will stop in a British shop
and grab a cup of tea.
She takes a stroll on the North Sea coast.
Puffins and gulls she can see.
She then goes south toward France and Spain
and east toward Italy.

Western Europe

ICELAND

Atlantic Ocean

UNITED KINGDOM

NETHERLANDS

DENMARK

North Sea

IRELAND

BELGIUM

GERMANY

LUXEMBOURG

Bay of Biscay

FRANCE

SWITZERLAND

Adriatic Sea

PORTUGAL

Ligurian Sea

ITALY

SPAIN

Mediterranean Sea

Wendy

ICELAND

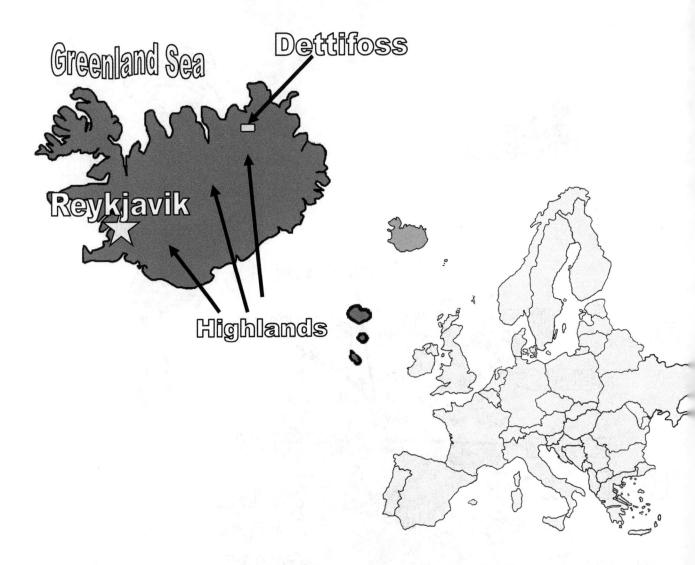

The highlands of Iceland are cold and mostly uninhabited mountains. Dettifoss is the largest waterfall in Europe. Iceland is often considered to be part of the region of Scandinavia.

Rey loves Iceland, its highlands so cold.
He loves reading sagas, and stories of old.
So many volcanoes and geysers abound.
The largest of waterfalls also are found.
Black pudding and shark heads
will Rey often eat.
But sheep liver sausage
is Rey's favorite treat.

Reykjavik
"Rey"

IRELAND

Atlantic Ocean

Irish Sea

Dublin

Celtic Sea

Isle of Man

Ireland is the biggest zinc producer in Europe. The Gaelic people are predominant in Ireland, the Scottish Highlands, and the Isle of Man.

Northern Ireland (U.K.)

Ireland

Belfast

Dublin

Little Miss
Dublin

Dublin's love of stepdance
makes her feet so fast and free.
It is a lovely remnant
of her Gaelic ancestry.
Her native tongue is Irish,
which she speaks most everywhere.
She also knows her English
and she'll use it here and there.
Her friends in Northern Ireland,
belong to the U.K.
She visits them in Belfast through
the Northern Ireland Railway.

UNITED KINGDOM

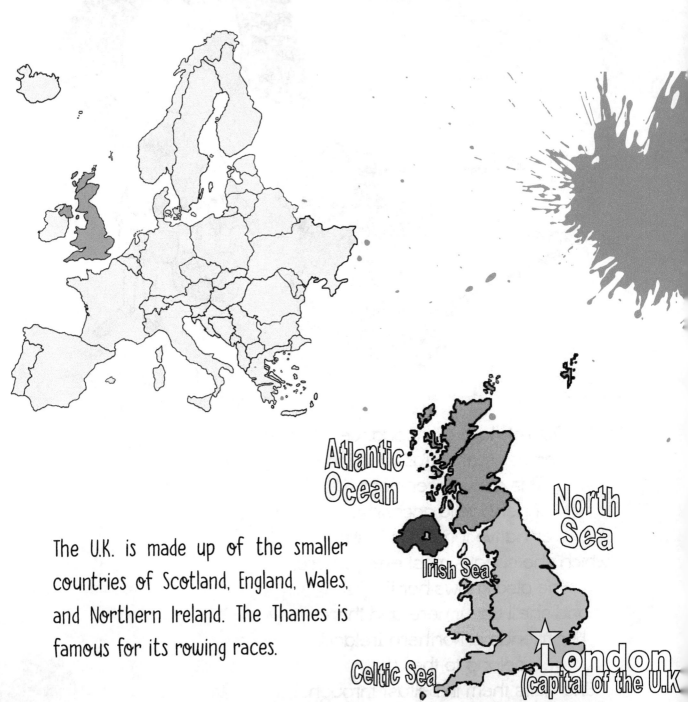

The U.K. is made up of the smaller countries of Scotland, England, Wales, and Northern Ireland. The Thames is famous for its rowing races.

Atlantic Ocean

North Sea

Irish Sea

Celtic Sea

London (capital of the U.K

English Channel

River Thames

London

Countries of Great Britain

Scotland

Edinburgh

Belfast

Northern Ireland

Wales

Cardiff

London

England

London

The highlands in Scotland and hill walking boots
remind little London of his Scottish roots.
In Wales he plays football and rugby, great games!
In England he visits the great River Thames.
He thinks of all things that Great Britain's done well:
Inventors like Newton and Darwin and Bell.
For writers and poets, there are an awful lot:
There are Shakespeare and Dickens and Sir Walter Scott.

DENMARK

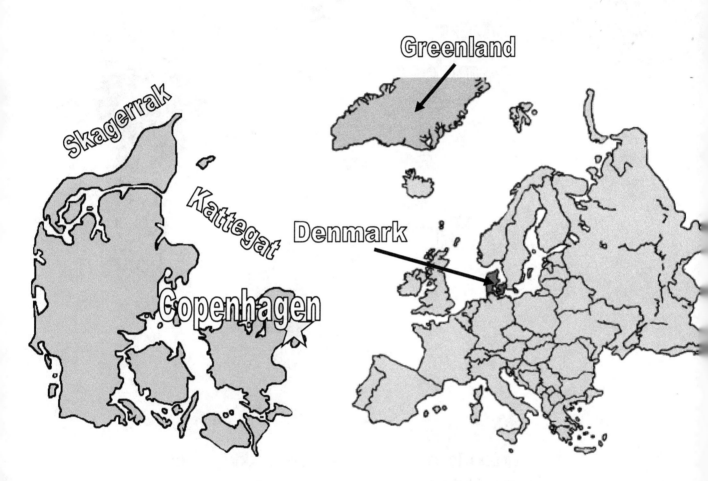

Greenland is an autonomous country within the Kingdom of Denmark. The Little Mermaid is a famous statue based on a tale by Hans Christian Anderson.

Miss Copenhagen loves her home,
its peace and equality.
Its windmills and brick houses
add to its tranquility.
Great Danish writers left behind
great works that everyone knows.
The Ugly Ducking is one of them,
as is The Emperor's New Clothes.

Little Miss Copenhagen

NETHERLANDS

North Sea

Amsterdam ★

The Netherlands is one of the seven kingdoms in Europe. The others are Sweden, Norway, U.K., Denmark, Belgium, and Spain. The Netherlands is often called "Holland."

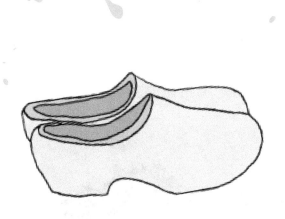

Miss Amsterdam is very tall
and speaks in fluent Dutch.
Windmills, wooden shoes and cheese
are things she loves so much.
Tomatoes, apples, chilis, bulbs
and flowers she does grow.
And for fun she goes to look
at paintings by van Gogh.

Miss Amsterdam

BELGIUM

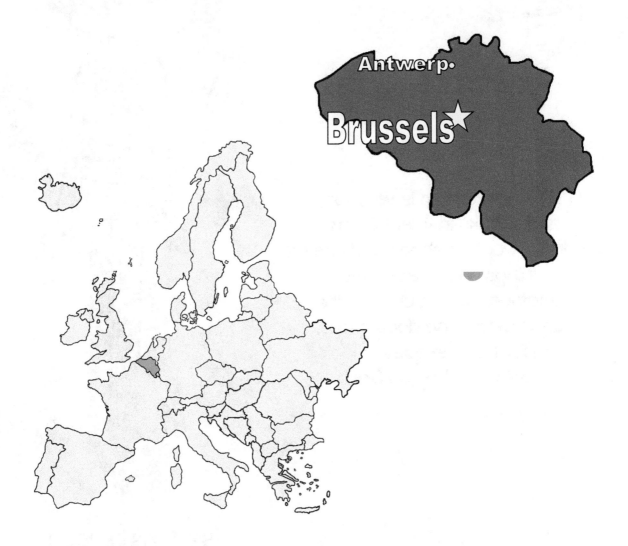

Antwerp.

Brussels ★

Belgium has three different languages: Dutch,
French, and German. French fries originated in
Belgium. Antwerp is a famous northern city in
Belgium.

Some of Brussels' friends speak French,
while some speak only Dutch.
As to which she likes herself,
she doesn't care so much.
Brussels loves her waffles
and her chocolate and french fries.
There is a store in Antwerp
where these foods are what she buys.

Little Miss
Brussels

LUXEMBOURG
(Grand Duchy of Luxembourg)

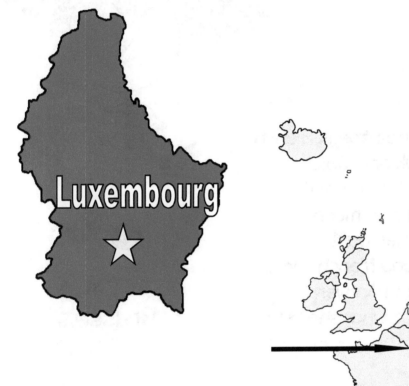

The Red lands are Luxembourg's industrial heartland. Luxembourg is the world's only Grand Duchy, or a country that is led by a Grand Duke or Duchess.

Little Miss Luxembourg
heads toward big towns.
They're found in The Red Lands,
which have reddish grounds.
She speaks Luxembourgish,
and French, c'est la vie.
She also knows German.
She's great at all three.
As Grand Duchies go,
this one might get lonely.
'Cause in all the world,
this country's the only.

Little Miss
Luxembourg

Luxembourg
★

Pétange
Differdange
Esch

Towns of
The Red Lands

GERMANY

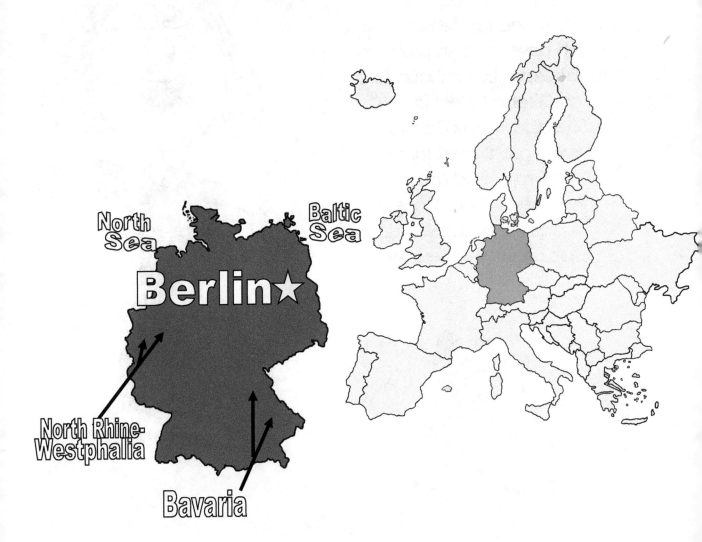

Dusseldorf is capital of the German state of North Rhine-Westphalia. Munich is the capital of Bavaria, renowned for its culture. Other important cities include Hamburg and Frankfurt.

Berlin's always active and she
travels round the clock.
She listens on a high speed train
to Wagner, Brahms and Bach.
To Munich and to Dusseldorf
she quickly makes her way.
Except for now it's Beethoven
that she is letting play.
After a day at the local zoo
and then a wildlife park,
her mother reads Rapunzel from
the Brother's Grimm at dark.

Berlin

SWITZERLAND

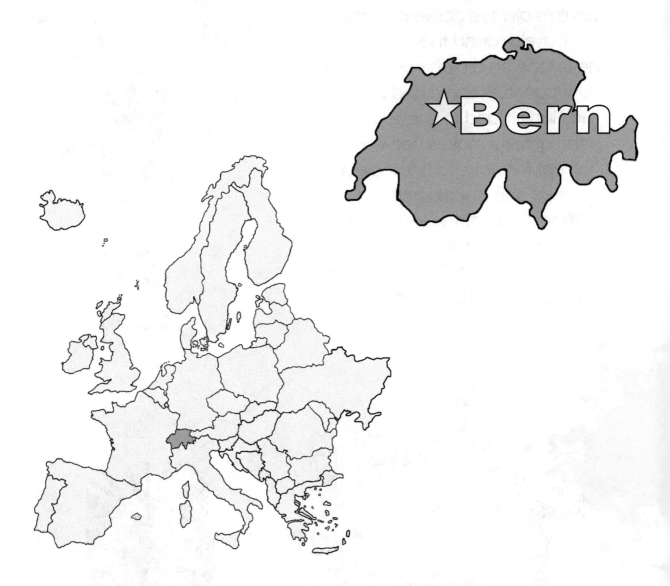

★Bern

Lake Geneva is the largest lake in Switzerland. Fondue is a popular dish in Switzerland.

Little Miss Bern
hikes the Alps in the south.
She pops some Swiss chocolates
in her tiny mouth.
To fine Lake Geneva
she'll go in the west,
with scrumptious Swiss Fondue,
which she likes the best.
Of skiing and yodeling
she'll never grow weary...
The story of Heidi
does make her quite teary.

Little Miss
Bern

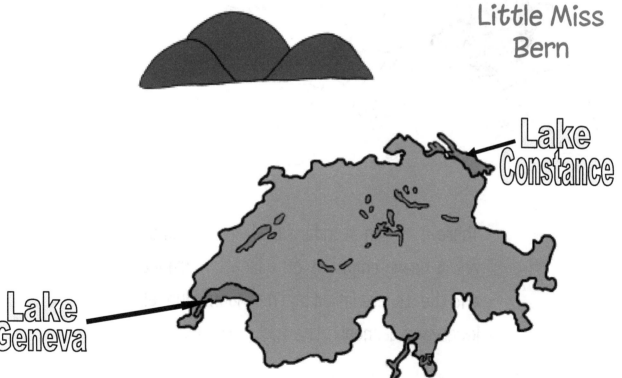

Lake
Constance

Lake
Geneva

FRANCE

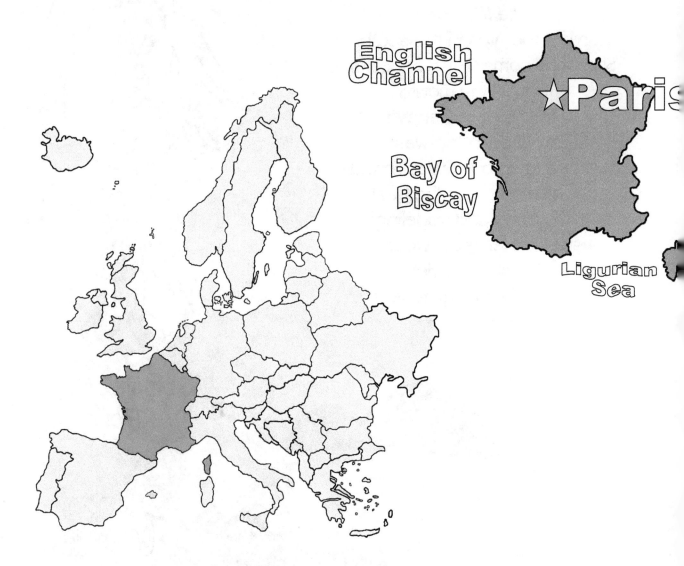

English Channel

Bay of Biscay

★Paris

Ligurian Sea

There is a high standard of living in France and a heavy emphasis on education. France and the U.K. are linked by the Channel Tunnel, located underneath the English Channel.

Paris

Paris has a lot to show
the tourists that come by:
The Eiffel Tower, Louvre,
and the Palace of Versailles.
Paris has a family that is very well to do.
They make sure she acts ladylike
and does her best in school.
The Channel Tunnel Paris takes
to sometimes get away.
It stretches all the way from France
and reaches the U.K.

SPAIN

Bay of
Biscay

Madrid
★

Majorca

Strait of Gibraltar

Paella is a rice-based dish that reflects Spain's strong Mediterranean influence. Don Quixote, written by the Spanish author Miguel de Cervantes, is considered the first modern novel.

Madrid walks the high plateaus
of her beloved Spain.
She ventures up the mountains north
where there is a lot of rain.
She loves flamenco dancing,
and paella's fun to eat.
Don Quixote is her all-time
favorite book to read.

Little Miss
Madrid

PORTUGAL

Atlantic Ocean

Lisbon

Northern Portugal is mainly mountainous, whereas southern Portugal has mostly rolling plains. Portugal is among countries with the highest fish consumption per person.

Azores

Madeira

Little Miss Lisbon

Lisbon walks through mountains north
and speaks in Portuguese.
The air is clear and weather's warm.
The fish are caught with ease.
Madeira and the Azores west
are islands big and full,
despite being so far away
belong to Portugal.

ITALY

Adriatic Sea

☆Rome

Mediterranean Sea

Pompeii is a town-city that was destroyed by a volcanic eruption in the days of the Roman Empire. A piazza is a city square. Opera was born in Italy around the year 1600 AD.

Little Rome finds much to do
with lots for him to see:
Piazzas and the Pompeii ruins,
and isle of Sicily.
An opera house in Naples,
and, in Milan, a big church,
are some of what Rome comes across
as he goes on his search.
His father loves espresso,
with a pasta dish as well.
He grows fine grapes for making wine
which he can also sell.

Rome

Milan

Naples

Sardinia

Sicily

Meandering through the Microstates with Mickey

Mickey

(Germany)

(France)

(Austria)

Liechtenstein

(Switzerland)

Pyrenees Mtns

Monaco

San Marino

Vatican City

(Italy)

(Portugal)

Andorra

(Spain)

Malta

While the rest of his friends
visit countries they know,
Mickey wonders where HE should go.
The Microstates are the places he picks,
with five principalities and small republics.
He'll then finish up in the Vatican City—
To miss that for sure would have been a pity!
Andorra's the largest of all of these.
It's found way up high in the Pyrenees.
Mickey then travels to small Liechtenstein,
far up in the Alps, near the start of the Rhine.
He flies out to Malta, an isle in the sea.
It's not all that far off from Italy.
Next is fine Monaco, where he sees a casino.
Then the old old Republic of San Marino.
And lastly he visits St. Peter's, so tall,
in Vatican City, the smallest of all.

Trapsing through the Transcontinental Countries with Tricia

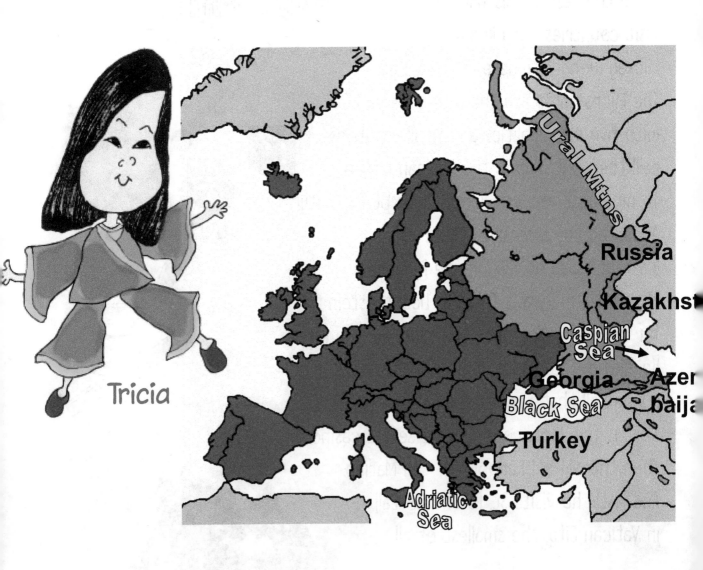

Tricia

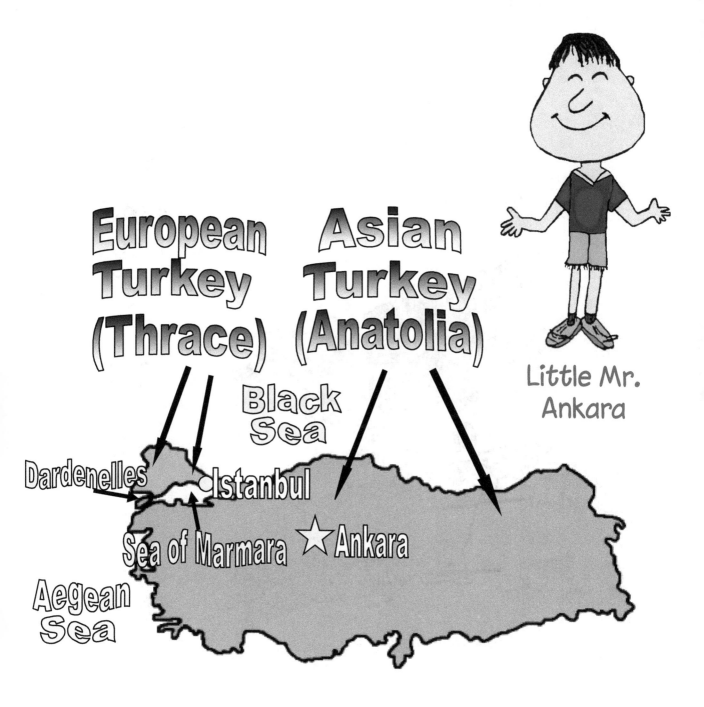

European Turkey (Thrace)

Asian Turkey (Anatolia)

Little Mr. Ankara

Black Sea

Dardenelles

Istanbul

Sea of Marmara ⭐Ankara

Aegean Sea

In Turkey, Europe is separated from Asia first by the
Dardenelles Strait, then by the Sea of Marmara,
and finally by the Bosporus, or Strait of Istanbul.
The city of Istanbul lies on both continents.

Georgia

Black Sea

Tbilisi ★

Greater Caucasus Mountains

European Georgia

Asian Georgia

Lesser Caucasus Mountains

Little Mr. Tbilisi

Many geographers say that the European-Asian border in Georgia is the valley between the Greater and Lesser Caucasus Mountains.
This makes Tbilisi a transcontinental capital, and places over half of Georgia in Europe.

Azerbaijan

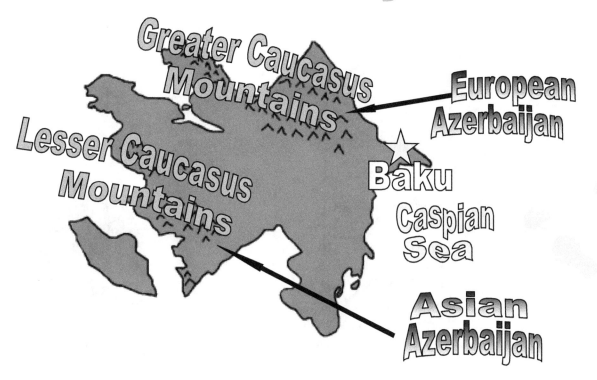

Greater Caucasus Mountains

Lesser Caucasus Mountains

European Azerbaijan

★ Baku

Caspian Sea

Asian Azerbaijan

As in Georgia, the border between Europe and Asia in Azerbaijan is the river valley between the two Caucasus ranges. About half of Azerbaijan is therefore located in Europe.

Little Mr. Baku

Kazakhstan

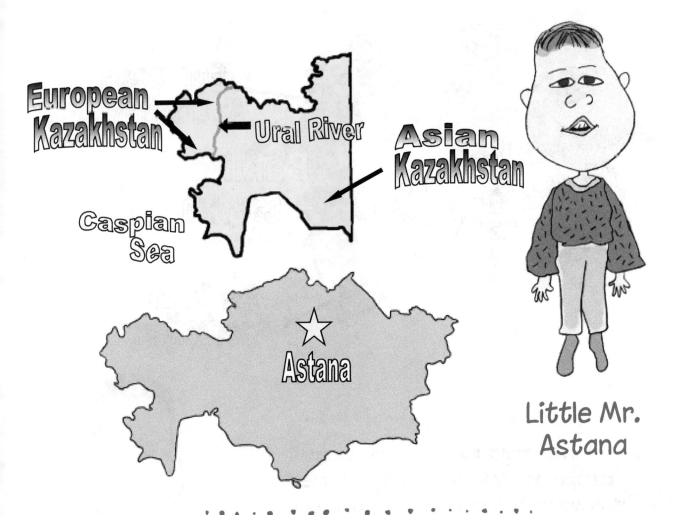

European Kazakhstan

Ural River

Asian Kazakhstan

Caspian Sea

★ Astana

Little Mr. Astana

Geographers often claim that the Ural River forms the border between Europe and Asia in Kazakhstan. Only about 5% of the country is located in Europe, and politically, Kazakhstan is mainly an Asian country.

Russia

Little Miss Moscow

The Ural Mountains are usually considered the continental border in Russia. Only one-fifth of Russia is west of the Urals, but this area is larger than all of Western Europe!

Russia boasts the tallest mountain, Mount Elbrus, the longest river, the Volga, and the largest lake, Ladoga, in Europe.

Through Europe we went, a splendid journey with Stevie, Wendy, and their friend, Ernie. And Tricia and Mickey had joined the three, between the Atlantic and Caspian Sea.

From huge, huge Russia to the Vatican City, they found many places both rugged and pretty. Like the Ural Mountains, so tall and vast that sit in the east and are hard to get past... Or the icy shores of the Barents Sea and triangular island of Sicily.

The five friends meet with back packs in hand to explore once again this incredible land.

CPSIA information can be obtained
at www.ICGtesting.com
Printed in the USA
LVHW061424040422
715262LV00009B/444

9 781642 557787